i-SPY

garden challenge

DO IT! SCORE IT!

Published by Collins
An imprint of HarperCollins Publishers
Westerhill Road, Bishopbriggs, Glasgow G64 2QT
www.harpercollins.co.uk

HarperCollins Publishers
Macken House, 39/40 Mayor Street Upper, Dublin 1, D01 C9W8, Ireland

A catalogue record for this book is available from the British Library.

ISBN 9780008562632

Printed in the UAE

10 9 8 7 6 5 4 3 2 1

Text by Heather Ryce
Front cover image © RimDream/Shutterstock.com
Internal images: p33, p60, p66, p67 (top) courtesy of Jennifer Smith and Oliver Smith;
p64 courtesy of Heather Ryce; p88 © DonSmith/Alamy Stock Photo; all other images
© Shutterstock.com

i-SPY

garden challenge

DO IT! SCORE IT!

Contents

Tick off
each activity
as you do it!

How to use this book

Get ready to take on the i-SPY challenge with 50 activities to get closer to nature!

Once you've done each activity tick it off on the contents list. You can do them in any order you like.

Note to grown-up: Join in the fun by doing the activities together and supervise any that you feel necessary.

Look out for activities which have eco points. These are awarded for doing something that helps look after the planet and its wildlife. Once you score 200 eco points, send off for your i-SPY eco-hero certificate and badge.

As well as activities, the book is packed with facts, photos and things to spot. If you spy it, score it by ticking the circle or star. Items with a star are difficult to spot so you'll have to search high and low to find them. Once you score 1000 spotter points, send off for your i-SPY super-spotter certificate and badge.

How to get your i-SPY certificates and badges

✓ Ask a grown-up to check your score.

✓ Apply for your certificate and badge at collins.co.uk/i-SPY (if you are under the age of 13 you'll need a parent or guardian to do this).

✓ We'll send you your certificate and badge!

Water your garden

During summer, when there is less rain, help the flowers in your garden by watering them.

You'll need:

watering can or recycled plastic bottle

What to do:

1 Push your fingers down into the soil. If the soil feels dry, it's time to water your flowers.

2 The best time to water the garden is first thing in the morning. This lets the water soak deep into the soil before it evaporates from the heat of the day.

3 Water the base of flowers. Avoid putting too much water on the leaves or fruits to help prevent diseases that like moisture.

Fruit and vegetables need to be watered regularly for them to grow. If you have some growing in your house or garden, make sure they are well watered.

See if you can spot these flowers when you are watering the garden.

Lavender
5 POINTS

Hydrangea
15 POINTS

Sunflower
5 POINTS

Coneflower
20 POINTS

Peony
20 POINTS

Rose
10 POINTS

Make leaf mulch

Removing dead leaves that have fallen to the ground at the end of summer ensures that sufficient sunlight and moisture reach the grass and soil below. The material you collect can be recycled into mulch to help your garden grow the next year.

You'll need:

brush and shovel, rake (if you have one), gardening gloves, black bin bag, scissors, watering can

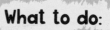

What to do:

1 Use a rake or your hands to put dead leaves into mounds. If you are using your hands, wear gardening gloves.

2 Recycle a large plastic bin bag to store your leaves. Ask an adult to help you cut small holes in the bottom of the bag for drainage.

3 Place the leaves into the bin bag and then pour water over the top, letting it drain out the bottom.

4 Tie your bag in a knot and store it somewhere safe, like a shed or garage.

Over the next six months the leaves will decompose. When it is spring, you can add your leaf mulch to any soil where plants are. The mulch will help stop your soil from drying out and reduce the number of weeds that grow. It will also make your garden look fresh and boost the nutrients in the soil.

Can you spot these spring flowers growing when you are putting your leaf mulch in the soil?

Daffodil

10 POINTS

Snowdrop

10 POINTS

Primrose

5 POINTS

Crocus

15 POINTS

Tulip

10 POINTS

Score 20 eco points for using recycled leaf mulch to help your spring garden grow.

20 ECO POINTS

Bring your plants inside

Some plants, known as tender plants, don't survive cold temperatures and need to be moved indoors during the winter.

You'll need:

gardening gloves, mats or old towels

What to do:

1. Check with an adult what plants need to be brought inside. Then prepare an area inside to keep your plants safe until spring. Lay down mats or old towels near a window so your floor will be protected, and your plants will still be in the light.

2. Before bringing your plants inside, check the leaves and soil for any insects or snails. Gently remove them and leave them in the garden near to where your plants were.

3. Remember to water your plants regularly during the winter. When the temperature increases and spring approaches, you can put them back outside.

Score 10 eco points for protecting tender plants all year round.

10 ECO POINTS

Plant bulbs for next year

A great job for the start of winter is to plant bulbs, ready for them to blossom in the spring.

You'll need:

gardening gloves, trowel, bulbs, watering can

What to do:

1 Choose some bulbs to plant with an adult, such as daffodils and tulips.

2 Bulbs prefer drier soil. Prod the soil with your finger; if it feels dry, you can plant your bulbs in the ground.

3 Ask an adult to help you dig a hole using a trowel. Your hole should be about 2–3 times as deep as your bulb is tall. Put your bulb into the hole and cover it with soil. Then pat it flat.

4 Plant the bulbs with the pointy-end up and the roots facing down.

5 Give them a good soak with your watering can.

6 Wait a few months until spring arrives. Then watch your flowers grow!

You can also plant bulbs in pots. Keep the pots outside for a few weeks during winter to help make sure the bulbs flower in spring.

Identify birds in your garden

Gardens are a great place to identify different birds, as a range of species will visit throughout the day.

Blackbird (male)

10 POINTS

Blackbird (female)

10 POINTS

Chaffinch

15 POINTS

TOP SPOT!

Greenfinch

40 POINTS

Greenfinch have declined in number due to a parasite-induced disease that stops them from feeding properly. To help, make sure you keep your bird feeders clean (see page 17).

Starling

15 POINTS

Nuthatch

25 POINTS

Song thrush

20 POINTS

Wren

20 POINTS

Jackdaw

10 POINTS

Magpie

10 POINTS

Woodpigeon

10 POINTS

Watch birds in your garden

Watch the different birds in your garden and note down what they are doing.

You'll need:

notepad, pen, binoculars

What to do:

1 Find a quiet space in your garden or by a window. Make yourself comfy, as you may be sitting a while before you see a bird.

2 When you spot a bird, write down the date, time, weather and what bird you think you saw. Also make a note of how many birds of the same species you see and what they were doing. For example, were they feeding, bathing or fighting?

3 Watch the birds in your garden on different days and at different times.

4 Keep a record of the birds you see throughout the year.

Why not join in with the RSPB's Big Garden Birdwatch, which takes place every January? Be part of one of the world's largest wildlife surveys! All you need to do is sit for an hour and record what birds you see in your garden. Find out more at the RSPB's website.

Clean your bird feeders

If you have bird feeders in your garden, it is important to clean them regularly. This helps to stop diseases being transmitted to wild birds feeding from them.

You'll need:

bucket of warm, soapy water,
cleaning brush, dry cloth,
antibacterial soap

What to do:

1 First, remove any uneaten or old food from the bird feeder to stop the build-up of bacteria.

2 Soak the feeder in a bucket of warm, soapy water and scrub it thoroughly with a brush. Then rinse the soap away with fresh tap water.

3 Dry the bird feeder by leaving it to air dry or by using a clean cloth.

4 Wash your hands with antibacterial soap. When the feeder is completely dry, refill it with fresh food.

You should clean your bird feeders around once a week depending on the weather and the number of birds that use them.

Make fat balls for birds

Birds love energy-rich fat balls, especially during winter.

You'll need:

bowl, spoon, food scraps, porridge oats, lard, frying pan, yogurt pots, scissors, string

What to do:

1 Add into a bowl the dry mixture of porridge oats and food scraps.

2 With the help of an adult, melt the lard. Add this into your bowl (around two parts lard to one part dry mixture) and mix everything together.

3 Ask an adult to pierce holes in the bottom of the yogurt pots. Thread the string through each hole, leaving a few inches draped over the top.

4 Turn your yogurt pots over and spoon in the mixture. Leave enough string at the top and bottom to hang your fat balls.

5 Place the filled yogurt pots in the fridge overnight to set.

6 Cut the yogurt pots from your fat balls with the help of an adult. Double check that there is no plastic on them.

7 Tie a knot on one side of each string to secure the fat balls. Then hang them in a tree or beside a window.

These birds enjoy eating fat balls. Can you spot them in your garden?

Great tit

15 POINTS

Long-tailed tit

20 POINTS

Woodpecker

TOP SPOT!

40 POINTS

Blackcap

25 POINTS

Score 20 eco points for using leftover kitchen scraps to feed garden birds.

20 ECO POINTS

Make a buffet table for birds

Why not turn a whole patch of your garden into a buffet area for birds? You are going to make monkey nut skewers, a peanut butter roller and dried bird mix.

You'll need:

an old tray, monkey nuts, unsalted peanuts, raisins, fruit such as apples, pears or berries, peanut butter, bird seed, string, scissors, butter knife/spoon, toilet or kitchen rolls, bowl

What to do:

1 Lay out the items around the tray, so you can see clearly what you have.

2 With the help of an adult, use the scissors to poke small holes through the middle of ten monkey nuts. Then thread a piece of string through each shell. Securely tie one end of the string in a knot. These are your monkey nut skewers.

3 Next, ask an adult to make a small hole near the top and bottom of a toilet or kitchen roll. Coat the whole roll in peanut butter with your knife or spoon. When the toilet roll is coated, roll it in bird seed so it sticks firmly onto the peanut butter. Thread a piece of string through the holes and tie it securely so it can hang in your garden. This is your peanut butter roller.

4 Add nuts, raisins and any fruit or berries into a bowl. Stir the mixture. This is your dried bird mix.

5 Place everything onto the tray and take it outside. Many birds don't like to eat in the open, so hanging the food in a sheltered area may encourage more birds to your buffet.

6 Hang your skewers and the peanut butter roller to tree branches and on shrubs. Scatter the dried bird mix on a bird table or on the ground beneath. While many birds don't mind hanging onto feeders, some birds such as robins and blackbirds prefer to eat on a table or on the ground. By placing your food items at different heights, you are catering to different bird species.

7 Remember to tidy up any leftover food from your buffet at the end of each day to deter rodents from your garden.

Make a bird bath

Providing water in your garden for birds helps them stay hydrated and cool in the summer. It is also a good water source for them in the winter, when many of their natural watering holes are frozen.

Bird baths attract more species of birds to your garden. Even if some birds aren't interested in the food in your feeders or the bird buffet, they might visit just to go for a dip!

You'll need:

large shallow bowl such as a circular plant tray, smooth stones or pebbles, four bricks or large stones, watering can or recycled plastic bottle

What to do:

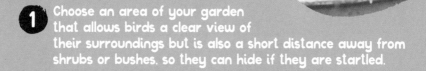

1 Choose an area of your garden that allows birds a clear view of their surroundings but is also a short distance away from shrubs or bushes, so they can hide if they are startled.

2 With the help of an adult, place the bricks or stones on the ground and lay the large shallow bowl on top, making sure it is stable and won't tip easily. Providing a raised bird bath helps birds see their surroundings a little better.

3 Put the smooth stones or pebbles in your bird bath, so birds have something to grip when they are bathing or drinking.

4 Fill your bird bath with cool, clean water from your watering can or bottle. The RSPB recommend that bird baths are no deeper than 10 cm, so keep that in mind when filling your bath.

5 Find a good viewing spot. Then enjoy watching birds and other wildlife drink and bathe in the water.

6 Clean your bird bath regularly to stop birds becoming ill from disease or dirty water.

See if you can spot any of these birds having a drink or a bath!

Blue tit

5 POINTS

Robin

10 POINTS

House sparrow

10 POINTS

Make a bird house

A bird house is a great way to watch nesting birds and fledglings (young birds) throughout spring and summer. This activity requires sharp tools, so ask an adult for help.

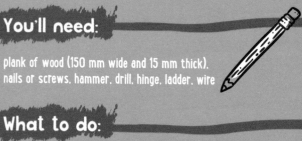

You'll need:

plank of wood (150 mm wide and 15 mm thick),
nails or screws, hammer, drill, hinge, ladder, wire

What to do:

1 Ask an adult to cut sections of the plank of wood to create a small nest box, complete with sloping roof and entrance/exit hole. The RSPB website has information packs you can download. The size of the entrance/exit hole to your bird house will determine what kind of bird will nest in it – the bigger the hole, the bigger the bird. A recommended size is 30 mm, but visit the RSPB website for more information.

2 The inside of the box should be 100 mm square by around 150 mm tall. The entrance/exit hole should be cut two thirds of the way up from the bottom of the box to stop predators reaching inside or fledglings jumping out too early.

3 Ask an adult to make a small drainage hole in the base of the box with a drill to keep the inside nice and dry.

4 With the help of an adult, use galvanised nails or screws (ones that are coated with a protective metallic layer) to put your wooden box together.

5 Create a hinged lid on the bird house so you can clean it out easily in autumn when birds have finished nesting. Birds typically nest between March and August, so never disturb or clean out the bird house then.

6 When the bird house is complete, ask an adult to put it on a tree or fence post around 3–5 metres from the ground and secure it with wire. Make sure the bird house is sheltered from the wind and doesn't get too much sunlight. Tilt the box downwards so that rainwater can run off it.

If you are unable to make a bird house, don't worry! Many supermarkets, pet shops and home stores sell ones which you can put up in your garden.

Score 40 eco points for making a bird house for nesting birds and fledglings.

40 ECO POINTS

Use natural ways to control pests

Some people use chemicals called pesticides to control pests. Unfortunately they can be harmful to other plants and animals, and don't just target pests. Natural ways to control pests are better for humans, wildlife and the environment.

You'll need:

salt, kettle, hard-bristled scrubbing brush, spray bottle, detergent, eggshells

What to do:

1 If weeds are difficult to remove, cover them with two tablespoons of salt. Then, with the help of an adult, pour boiled water over the weeds. When the area has cooled, scrub the weeds away with a scrubbing brush.

2 Spray leaves which are covered in aphids with warm, soapy water. Squeeze some detergent into a spray bottle and add warm water, then give the bottle a shake.

3 If slugs are eating plants in your garden, use eggshells to protect them! Put old, cracked eggshells around the plant you want to protect, with the round section of the shell in the ground and the jagged edge facing upwards. Slugs won't eat the plant to avoid hurting themselves on the sharp edges of the eggshell.

Some animals in your garden will prey on garden pests.
See if you can spot these natural predators.

Ladybird

10 POINTS

Frog

20 POINTS

Lacewing

TOP SPOT!

Hedgehog

40 POINTS

20 POINTS

Score 20 eco points for using natural ways to control pests rather than pesticides.

20 ECO POINTS

Identify weeds in your garden

Weeds are fast-growing plants that grow in places they are not wanted. They grow well in most types of soil. They are considered pests because they take space and nutrition from other plants.

Weeds grow faster in warm weather, so removing them during summer is necessary to keep your garden healthy. Being able to identify weeds means you can tackle them quicker and help keep your garden full of different types of flowers.

There are three main types of weed: annual, perennial and tough weeds. Can you spot them in your garden or at the park?

1 Annual weeds can spread rapidly in your garden by seed. However, they are easy to remove as their roots are neither strong nor long.

Chickweed

Hairy bittercress

10 POINTS

15 POINTS

2 Perennial weeds can be hard to reduce as they spread by seed as well as by their roots. You must remove every part of the weed to ensure it does not grow back and this can be hard to do by hand. Using organic methods, like salt and hot water (see page 26), can help tackle these plants.

Couch grass

5 POINTS

Nettles

10 POINTS

3 Tough weeds are hardy versions of perennial weeds. They regrow from the smallest piece of root left behind in the soil. Usually, the only effective way to remove them is to use a very strong chemical weedkiller.

Japanese knotweed

20 POINTS

Horsetail

25 POINTS

Score 15 eco points for saving dandelions in your garden. Dandelions begin to flower at the same time that bees emerge from hibernation. It is a great species for bees to get nectar and pollen early in spring.

15 ECO POINTS

Identify pesky pests

All animals have their place in the food chain. You should never completely remove a pest from its natural environment, as this could lead to an imbalance, but it can be helpful to manage a species of animal or plant if there are too many of them.

See if you can spot these garden pests.

Snail
5 POINTS

Slug
5 POINTS

Aphid
10 POINTS

Cabbage moth caterpillar
15 POINTS

Leafhopper
20 POINTS

Spider mite
20 POINTS

Feed hedgehogs

Hedgehogs have declined in numbers due to habitat loss (there is less space for them to survive and reproduce) and the use of pesticides. The best way to encourage hedgehogs into your garden and help protect them is to feed them.

A hedgehog eats slugs, beetles, worms, caterpillars and millipedes, but you can offer them a little treat!

You'll need:

plate, shallow bowl, fork, dry or wet cat food

What to do:

1. Put some dry or wet cat food onto an old plate. Separate any large clumps into small pieces.

2. Provide clean water alongside the plate of food in a shallow bowl.

3. Put the food and water in a sheltered area of your garden, so the hedgehog can eat safely. You can watch it from a nearby window.

Avoid feeding hedgehogs:

- bread and milk – bread is not nutritious to a hedgehog and milk will give them an upset tummy

- mealworms – studies have shown that they can be very harmful to hedgehogs and even fatal in some cases.

Build a hedgehog highway

The average hedgehog travels around 2 km each night to find food. A great way to help hedgehogs move in and out of your garden is to build a hedgehog highway. An adult should help you with this activity.

You'll need:

saw, spade, soil pipe

What to do:

1 If you have a garden that is fenced in, ask an adult to saw a small hole at the base of the fence to allow access for a hedgehog.

2 An adult can also dig a shallow trench under your fence using a spade, then put a soil pipe there to create a safe tunnel in and out of your garden. The pipe should be about 13 cm squared for a hedgehog to fit through comfortably.

3 If your garden is enclosed by a brick wall, remove one of the bricks at the bottom to allow a hedgehog to get in and out. Again, ask for help from an adult before doing this.

In 2019, planning guidelines were changed in some areas to require hedgehog highways to be included in new housing developments.

Make hedgehog highway signposts

Why not make your hedgehog highway even more effective by encouraging your neighbours to join in?

Hedgehog highway signposts will tell everyone passing by the gardens in your street why the fences have a hole at the bottom. This will stop people blocking up the holes.

You'll need:

wooden plaque, paint or pens, hammer and nails

What to do:

1 Use waterproof paint or pens to write signposts saying 'Hedgehog highway! Please keep clear'. Draw a hedgehog under the writing.

2 Ask an adult to attach your hedgehog signpost to your fence using a hammer and nail.

Score 30 eco points for registering your hedgehog highway on the Big Hedgehog Map's website. This helps provide information about the positive impact of hedgehog highways on hedgehog populations.

30 ECO POINTS

Build a bug hotel

A bug hotel provides a safe space for creepy crawlies to escape predators and raise their young.

You can build your hotel at any time of the year, but you will have the most natural resources to work with in autumn, when the leaves fall off the trees.

You'll need:

recycled wooden pallet/wooden box/cardboard box, toilet roll tubes, planks of wood/ old roof tiles/roofing felt, four bricks, sticks, leaves, dry grass, dead wood, pine cones, straw, waterproof paint, hammer and nails, wild bird seed

What to do:

1 Find a level spot in your garden away from vegetable patches.

2 Choose the location of your bug hotel depending on what insects you want to attract – bees like to be in the sun when resting, whereas beetles prefer cool, damp conditions.

3 Position the four bricks so that your hotel will be raised off the ground.

4 Next, place the wooden pallet or box onto the bricks. You could make a multi-storey hotel by layering wooden pallets or boxes on top of one another.

5 Fill the hotel with toilet roll tubes, dead wood, leaves, grass, sticks, pine cones and straw to create tunnels and crevices for your insects to hide in. Try to bundle each type of material together to create sections in your hotel for different insects to use.

6 You can give the hotel a roof by placing wooden planks on top of pallets or adding old roof tiles or roofing felt.

7 Sprinkle some wild bird seed in and around your hotel to entice insects to move in.

8 Name your hotel by painting a sign onto a plank of wood or piece of cardboard. Ask an adult to attach the sign with a hammer and nails.

Count worms in your garden

Earthworms are welcome visitors to your garden as they help to improve soil structure and nutrients in the soil, simply by moving and eating their way through it! Seeing worms in your soil is a good indicator of a healthy garden.

You'll need:

spade, tarpaulin, gardening gloves

What to do:

1. With the help of an adult, use the spade to dig a section of soft ground 30 cm by 30 cm and around 15 cm deep.

2. Place the section of ground on the tarpaulin and gently pull apart the soil.

3. Count how many worms you find. If there are ten or more, you have a healthy population in your garden and it is a sign that your soil is in good condition.

4. If you don't find any worms, it could mean that your soil needs some extra help. Try to reduce using pesticides, water your soil more regularly and add some organic matter to it, such as compost or manure.

Other kinds of invertebrates and insects live in or visit your garden, especially if you provide them with places to hide or their own bug hotel. Can you spot these bugs?

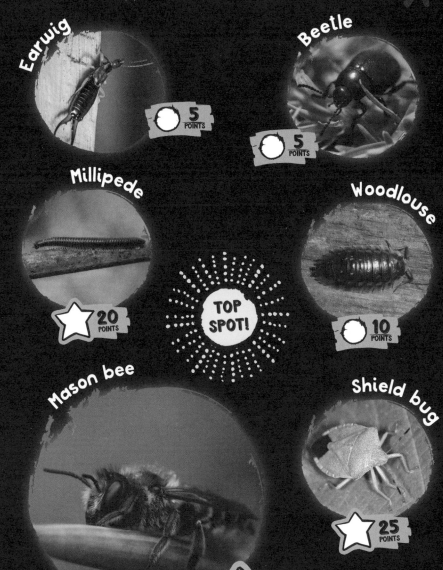

Earwig
5 POINTS

Beetle
5 POINTS

Millipede
20 POINTS

Woodlouse
10 POINTS

TOP SPOT!

Mason bee
40 POINTS

Shield bug
25 POINTS

Grow a bee-friendly garden

Bees play a crucial role in the environment because they pollinate plants.

However, bee populations are in trouble. Your garden could be a great habitat to help them.

Most bee species are active from March to October and are always on the lookout for nectar-rich plants. You can help your local bees by planting flowers in your garden between those months.

You'll need:

flowers to plant,
watering can

What to do:

1 Ask an adult if it is possible to include some bee-friendly plants in your garden. Flowers that bees love include marigolds, primroses and phacelias.

2 Water your flowers regularly through the warmer months of the year to keep them hydrated and healthy for visiting bees.

There are more than 250 species of bee in the UK, such as the bumblebee and honey bee. How many of these bees can you i-Spy?

Bumblebee

There are 24 species of bumblebee in the UK, including tree bumblebees and white-tailed bumblebees.

10 POINTS

Honey bee

Honey bees in the UK have gold bands across their bodies and black abdomens.

15 POINTS

Common carder bee

These bees are fluffy, brown and orange. They live in many different environments, including gardens, cities and parks.

30 POINTS

These bees live and feed on their own. Small holes in or near the ground in your garden could be a sign that a mining bee is nearby.

Tawny mining bee

TOP SPOT!

40 POINTS

Score 20 eco points for leaving an area of your garden untended. Some bees love long uncut grass and often make nests in undisturbed compost heaps.

20 ECO POINTS

Save a wasp nest

You might think of wasps as angry insects, always looking for someone to sting. This is not true! Wasps play a vital role in the ecosystem, controlling insect pests such as greenfly and some caterpillar species that would otherwise ruin our gardens. Wasps also help to pollinate plants, just like bees.

You might see a wasp nest on the ground or attached to tree branches or eaves of buildings. Wasps make their nests from chewed wood pulp and saliva. This makes them look like a ball of paper mache.

TOP SPOT!

40 POINTS

Score 10 eco points for leaving a wasp nest alone, as long as you have told an adult where it is and it is safe to do so. If you don't disturb a wasp nest, the risk of getting stung is low and your garden may benefit from additional predators and pollinators. The nest will eventually die off naturally when autumn arrives.

10 ECO POINTS

There are around 9,000 species of wasp in the UK! Some live in complex, social groups; others prefer to live by themselves. When you are in your garden, can you spot the following wasp species?

Common wasp

This species of wasp is most likely to disturb your summer barbecue! Common wasps build nests as big as footballs and have one single queen who produces between 6,000 and 10,000 worker wasps.

5 POINTS

European hornet

The European hornet is about two to three times larger than the common wasp. Their nests tend to be seen in tree cavities and even bird boxes.

20 POINTS

Red wasp

These wasps have a red tinge on their abdomen. Their nests are always built underground where a single queen lives with around 300 of her workers.

30 POINTS

Build a pond

A pond in your garden provides water for mammals, birds and insects, and offers a safe place for amphibians (small animals who live in water or a moist place). A pond is one of the best ways to help wildlife and to encourage species into your garden that you may not have seen before.

Your pond doesn't need to be huge or complex to attract wildlife. You can make one from almost any watertight container.

You'll need:

large watertight container such as a basin, a bucket, spade, stones, gravel, branches, aquatic plants

What to do:

1 Leave a bucket outside to collect rainwater. This may take a few days to fill up, so be patient.

2 Choose an area for your pond to be built – a sunny spot near the edge of your garden is a good location.

3 With the help of an adult, use the spade to dig a hole large enough to completely sink your container into the ground.

4 Fill your container with different-sized stones and branches. This creates different depths and helps any animals that have accidentally fallen in the pond to climb out.

5 Add your bucket of rainwater to the container. Avoid using tap water, which contains chemicals.

6 You could also add some aquatic plants to the container, for example water lilies. You don't need to do this, but it will improve the oxygen content and water quality of your pond. Always ask for help from an adult.

Score 40 points for building a pond. There are lots of environmental benefits in providing a water source in your garden, such as helping to look after different species of wildlife. You are a wildlife hero!

40
ECO
POINTS

Make a home for an amphibian

Amphibians include frogs, toads, newts and salamanders. They need to live in water or a moist habitat.

Over winter, many species of amphibian hibernate by going underground in damp soil or beneath piles of logs. This helps them to keep as warm as possible and avoid predators.

You can help amphibians through the cold months of the year by giving them a safe space in your garden.

You'll need:

spade, gardening gloves, stones, twigs or branches, leaf mulch (see page 10) or soil

What to do:

1 With the help of an adult, use the spade to dig a 30 cm deep hole in a shaded spot in your garden. If you have a pond, dig the hole near to that.

2 With your hands, shape the hole in the ground so it is nice and round (scoop the sides in a curved motion) and has a flat bottom.

3 Fill your hole with different-sized stones. Make sure the stones won't collapse onto each other but leave gaps for amphibians to squeeze themselves inside and bury down underneath.

4 Loosely pile leaf mulch or soil and some twigs or branches over the top of the hole until a small mound forms.

5 Leave a few small entrance holes so amphibians can enter easily.

6 Never disturb your amphibian home during winter as you may frighten an animal hiding inside.

Score 30 eco points for helping the amphibians in your garden. There are fewer amphibian species all over the world due to climate change, pollution and the loss of their homes. You are making a positive impact.

30 ECO POINTS

Identify amphibians in your garden

See how many of these amphibians you can spot in your garden.

The natterjack toad can only be found in around sixty places across the UK and is legally protected.

Natterjack toad

TOP SPOT!

40 POINTS

Common toad

10 POINTS

Smooth newt

35 POINTS

Common frog

10 POINTS

Palmate newt

25 POINTS

Great-crested newt

35 POINTS

In the UK, the great-crested newt is under serious threat from habitat loss. Like the natterjack toad, it is protected. So if you do spot one, don't disturb it and always keep your distance.

Have a tea party

During summer, enjoy your garden with friends. Remember to wear sun cream.

You'll need:

chairs/beanbags/cushions, table, tea set, plates and cutlery, cuddly toys

What to do:

1 With permission from an adult, invite some friends to your garden, or have a picnic with your cuddly toys.

2 Put out your tea set and cutlery. If you don't have a tea set, use cups or glasses and a jug.

3 Fill the plates with food or have a pretend tea party!

At the tea party, use your senses to:

10 POINTS

see something colourful

10 POINTS

hear birds

10 POINTS

smell something fresh

10 POINTS

touch something soft

10 POINTS

taste something sweet

Help a hungry butterfly

Unexpected cold weather or lack of flowers nearby can make young butterflies weak and hungry. Help a butterfly by giving it a sugary snack.

You'll need:

clean sponge, white sugar, spoon, bowl

What to do:

1 Make your sugar solution.
In a bowl, mix four parts of fresh, cool water with four parts of white sugar.

2 Soak one side of the sponge in the sugary solution from the bowl. Then place the dry side down on the ground in a sheltered area in your garden.

3 Carefully pick up the hungry butterfly by its wings, using your thumb and forefinger. Be very gentle.

4 Put the butterfly onto the wet side of the sponge and allow it to drink the sugar solution.

5 Notice if the butterfly feeds by unfurling what looks like a tube from its head. This is a bit like how we drink through a straw.

See if you can spot these butterflies in your garden or local park.

Painted lady

5 POINTS

Red admiral

5 POINTS

Small tortoiseshell

5 POINTS

Large white

5 POINTS

Peacock

5 POINTS

49

Climb a tree

Climbing trees is a great way to spend time outdoors and take in wonderful views. If you don't have trees in your garden, you could visit a local park.

Tree climbing is great exercise, and it can improve your confidence too when you see how high or long you can climb.

You'll need:

sturdy shoes, helmet if you haven't climbed before

What to do:

1 Always ask permission from an adult before you begin to climb and make sure someone is nearby when you are climbing.

2 If it's your first time, wear a helmet and start with a small tree that has stiff limbs which do not bend under your weight.

3 When you climb, push up with your legs to make it a little easier to reach the top.

4 Always have at least one stronghold – one hand or foot firmly positioned so that you feel secure in the tree.

5 Practise climbing down the tree before you go too high, so you get used to the different holds and positions on the way down.

Can you spot any of these trees in your garden or local park?

Wild cherry

15 POINTS

English oak

5 POINTS

Rowan

10 POINTS

Silver birch

15 POINTS

Hawthorn

15 POINTS

Create a fairy garden

If you want to attract some special visitors to your garden and create a fun outdoor space, why not make your own fairy garden?

You'll need:

large flowerpot, potting soil, pebbles, outdoor miniature flowers, fairy garden decorations

What to do:

1 Choose a place in your garden where you would like your fairy garden to grow. Ask an adult to help you put the flowerpot in that area.

2 Fill the flowerpot with soil and pat the top flat. Then, with the help of an adult, carefully plant the miniature flowers around the sides.

3 Use the pebbles to create mini paths or stairs for fairies to follow.

4 Finally, add decorations, such as a tiny table and chairs or a fairy house. How creative can you be?

5 Check your fairy garden each morning. Has anyone visited overnight?

When you are looking for fairies in your garden, can you spot these insects and plants?

You might see a dragonfly near water. They enjoy lying in the sun with their wings open.

20 POINTS

A damselfly is smaller than a dragonfly but looks similar.

25 POINTS

Dandelions use the wind to carry their seeds to a suitable patch of ground.

10 POINTS

TOP SPOT!

The hawthorn moth is rarely found north of Yorkshire.

40 POINTS

The goldcrest is the UK's smallest bird. You might see it darting in between trees and hedges looking for insects to eat.

30 POINTS

Walk barefoot on grass

Being in your garden is an amazing way to connect with nature. Use your senses to appreciate how your garden is full of life – from the sweet smell of flowers to the chirping birds at dawn, and all the different colours in autumn as the leaves start to fall.

Using your sense of touch by walking barefoot across grass can be a fun way to spend an afternoon. It has health benefits too, so get the whole family to join in!

You'll need:

bare feet

What to do:

1. Wait for a warm, sunny day to walk across the grass in your garden (or the park).

2. Take off your shoes and socks and stand still. How do the blades of grass feel under your feet? Close your eyes if it helps.

3. When you are used to the feeling, take a few steps. Does it feel different when you walk?

Did you know that walking barefoot can reduce swelling in sore legs and make the muscles of your feet stronger?

Be mindful in the garden

Mindfulness can boost your mood and improve your concentration. You can practise mindfulness anywhere, including your bedroom, the park and your garden.

You'll need:

a quiet place to sit, a blanket

What to do:

1. Find a quiet place in your garden and sit comfortably. If the weather is cool, wrap a blanket around you.

2. Close your eyes and focus on your breathing.

3. Clear your mind of any thoughts; just breathe in and out. Don't worry if your mind starts to wonder. Just notice that it has, then return your focus to your breath.

4. Take a few minutes each day to practise mindfulness. It may be difficult at first to clear your thoughts. Start by focusing for ten seconds, then twenty seconds and build from there.

5. Taking time each day to be present and mindful helps if you feel sad, angry or worried. It can increase energy levels too.

Have a sports day

Host your own sports day to bring family and friends together.

You'll need:

beanbags, balls, hula hoops and cones, rope, ribbon, supportive trainers

What to do:

1 Set up an obstacle course for two teams. If your garden isn't long, the teams can stand on the spot and complete challenges like who can hula hoop the longest.

2 Use an old piece of rope to play tug-of-war. Tie a ribbon in the centre of the rope. Then ask an equal number of people to line up at either end of the rope. Both teams pull as hard as they can when the referee says to start. The teams pull until the ribbon crosses where the referee is standing.

3 Put five hula hoops in a flat area of your garden, with some further away than others. Each player stands behind a line and throws three beanbags into the hula hoops. Each beanbag that lands in a hula hoop is worth points, depending on how far away the hula hoop is. The player with the most points wins!

Animals use their speed and strength to catch prey or avoid predators. Can you spot these animal athletes?

Foxes sometimes hunt by leaping high into the air and crashing down on unsuspecting prey.

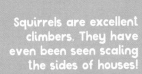
25
POINTS

Squirrels are excellent climbers. They have even been seen scaling the sides of houses!

10
POINTS

Swifts fly to the UK during the summer from Africa, hardly ever landing on the ground. They eat and even sleep on the wing – the ultimate endurance race!

25
POINTS

Make a bow and arrow

Setting targets in your garden to shoot with a bow and arrow is a fun activity you can do with friends or by yourself. Always ask permission from an adult first though, to check that the targets are safe to hit.

You can buy a bow and arrow from the shops, but you can also make one of your own, with the help of an adult.

You'll need:

plastic coat hanger, scissors, duct tape, elastic bands, pencils, card, glue

What to do:

1 Test the strength of your plastic coat hanger by tugging it firmly in different directions – if it feels like it could snap, it may not be strong enough to make your bow.

2 Ask an adult to carefully remove the hook of the hanger with a pair of scissors so you are left with a smooth bow shape.

3 Tightly wrap your bow in duct tape so all the plastic surface is covered.

4 Make the string of your bow. First, ask an adult to cut 3–5 strong elastic bands and tie them together to make one long band. Attach the elastic band string to your hanger, parallel to the straight section of the bow.

5 Make your arrows by wrapping pencils in duct tape. Leave the pointy tip of the pencil free.

6 Draw same-sized triangles on pieces of card and carefully cut them out. To make your arrowheads, sandwich the tip of the pencil in between two triangles and glue them together.

7 Test your bow by drawing an arrow back on the string and releasing it to hit a target.

Can you hit these targets?

A bullseye

10 POINTS

Something soft

10 POINTS

Something you can knock over

10 POINTS

33

Make a rainbow wood chime

If you don't have a garden where you can plant flowers, you can add colour by making a rainbow wood chime.

You'll need:

6-10 sticks, sandpaper, coloured acrylic paint, paintbrush, craft varnish, string, plastic lid

What to do:

1 With the help of an adult, snap or cut the sticks so they are all between 20 and 25 cm long. You can keep them all the same length or have different sizes.

2 Use sandpaper to make the sticks smooth.

3 Paint your sticks with different-coloured acrylic paint to create a rainbow of colours. The sticks may need a couple of coats of paint, so be patient.

4 When the paint is completely dry, coat the sticks with craft varnish. This will stop the paint from fading and chipping. Leave the sticks to completely dry.

5 Finally, pierce several holes in the plastic lid. Thread the string through each hole and attach to each stick. Gather the string at the top and tie to a low hanging branch or fence post in your garden. Then watch your rainbow wood chime dance in the wind!

Real rainbows are made up of seven colours – red, orange, yellow, green, blue, indigo and violet. They form when light from the sun is scattered by raindrops through a process known as refraction.

TOP SPOT!

Rainbow

15 POINTS

Double rainbow

30 POINTS

You might be lucky enough to spot a double rainbow!

34

Make a nature table

Creating a nature table is a great way to showcase interesting items you find in your garden.

You'll need:

a large tray, gloves, camera, bag

What to do:

1 Explore your garden and collect any interesting natural items, such as feathers, stones, leaves and sticks. Store them in a bag.

2 When you have gathered a range of items, arrange them on the tray to create your nature table.

3 If you don't know what an item is, look it up in a book or online.

4 Take a picture of the items you collected, or sketch them. How many different items did you manage to find?

5 Return the items where you found them.

How many of these items can you spot in your garden?

Pine cone
20 POINTS

Conker
15 POINTS

Feather
20 POINTS

TOP SPOT!

Bird egg
40 POINTS

Can you spot something that is...?

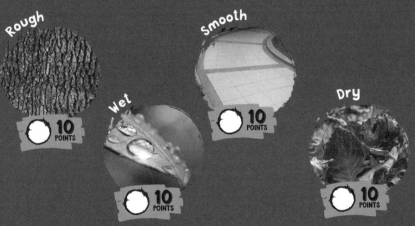

Rough
10 POINTS

Wet
10 POINTS

Smooth
10 POINTS

Dry
10 POINTS

Score 10 eco points for returning the items you find.

10 ECO POINTS

35

Make a stick maze

Gardens and other outdoor spaces have a variety of trees. Look out for different-sized sticks and branches; then challenge your friends and family by designing a stick maze!

You'll need:

lots of sticks and branches, stopwatch

What to do:

1 Collect lots of sticks and branches. The more you collect, the bigger and more complex your maze can be.

2 Find a large, flat area in your garden to build your maze.

3 Place sticks end to end to create paths. Remember to have lots of blocked ends so the maze isn't too simple to complete.

4 Get your friends or family members to take turns to complete the maze. Time how long they take; the winner is the person who gets to the end point the quickest.

It is useful to be able to identify the trees around you. Notice the size, colour and shape of the leaves.

When you are in your garden or out and about, can you spot these leaves?

Sycamore

5 POINTS

Ash

10 POINTS

Yew

15 POINTS

Willow

10 POINTS

Birch

5 POINTS

36

Make an egg carton greenhouse

Many people don't have the space or time to have a greenhouse in their garden. You can create your own mini greenhouse that will fit just about anywhere!

You'll need:

large plastic empty egg carton, large cardboard empty egg carton, potting soil, seeds such as basil or cress, scissors

What to do:

1 Remove any labels or paper from the egg carton.

2 With the help of an adult, cut the cardboard egg carton lid off. Then carefully cut out each individual egg pot. Trim their sides so they are small enough to comfortably fit into the grooves of the plastic egg carton. The plastic carton top should still be able to fully close. Make sure you recycle your egg carton afterwards.

3 With the help of an adult, pierce a hole through each plastic and cardboard egg pot to allow for extra drainage.

4 Fill each cardboard pot with soil and gently plant a seed in each. Water your newly planted seeds and close the plastic lid.

5 Leave in a warm, sunny spot and water regularly so the soil is always damp.

6 Wait until your seeds begin to sprout. You may have to leave the lid off after a while to give your seedlings more room to grow.

7 When the seedlings are big enough and the weather is nice, remove them from their cardboard egg pots and plant them in your garden. The cardboard will biodegrade in the soil.

Cress

Basil

Parsley

Rosemary

Score 30 eco points for growing any of the above herbs.

30 ECO POINTS

37

Take a flower apart

Taking a closer look at a flower can help us understand how they survive and how different they are from us.

There are many parts of a flower to learn about; we will look at the basic structures of most flowering plants.

You'll need:

scissors, tweezers, wooden chopping board or sturdy surface

What to do:

1. With the help of an adult, carefully cut a flower from the main part of the plant, including a few centimetres of stem. Always ask permission from an adult before removing flowers in your garden. Tulips, roses or daffodils are good flowers to dissect (take apart), as they have large flowering heads.

2. Put your flower head on a chopping board so that you can look at it more closely.

Petals are often brightly coloured to attract insects.

The stem is often hard and inflexible. Its job is to hold the flower up to face the sun.

A sepal is an outer ring of a flower that may look like green leaves or extra petals. Sepals help to protect the flower during the budding stage. A typical tulip has three petals and three sepals which all look like petals, whereas daffodil sepals are fused to the outer petals.

3 Gently peel back some petals with your tweezers so you can see the inside of the flower.

The stamen is the male part of the flower which produces pollen. It grows at the centre of the flower and has small, delicate stalks.

The pistil is the female part of the flower: it is the bit in the middle of the flower that produces the seeds.

38

Paint your own flowerpot

Painting flowerpots for your garden adds a personal, unique touch. They are also great presents to give to friends and family to add to their home or garden.

plain terracotta plant pots, cloth, acrylic paint, paintbrushes, marker pens

What to do:

1. Clean your empty plant pots with a damp cloth to remove any dirt or soil.

2. Use your paintbrushes and marker pens to create a design on your flowerpots. Or use your fingers!

3. When you have finished, leave the paint to completely dry before planting flowers into the pots.

4. Decorate your garden with your cool, personalised plant pots – why not take a picture?

You need some flowers to put in your flowerpot! There are over 300,000 species of flowering plants in the world, so it may take some time to find out about them all!

How many of these flowers can you i-Spy in your garden or local park?

Ox-eye daisy
10 POINTS

Foxglove
10 POINTS

Forget-me-not
15 POINTS

Marigold
10 POINTS

Honeysuckle
20 POINTS

Snake's head fritillary

TOP SPOT!

40 POINTS

39

Grow sunflowers

Sunflowers are beautiful and they are easy to grow. They usually flower in August, so you need to sow the seeds from around mid-April to the end of May.

You'll need:

sunflower seeds, gardening gloves, rake, trowel, watering can

What to do:

1 Choose a sunny patch of your garden that has good-quality soil.

2 Prepare the area by removing any weeds. Use a rake to break up any large clumps of soil.

3 Use a trowel (or your finger) to make a small hole in the soil about 2 cm deep and place your seed inside. Cover the hole up and water until the topsoil is damp. Be careful not to overwater your sunflower as it grows!

4 If you are planting more than one seed, leave a gap between them of about 10–15 cm to ensure each seed has room to grow.

5 If your sunflower begins to grow taller than you, you may need to give it some support. Tie a long stick or cane to the stem to keep it upright.

There are more than 70 varieties of sunflower. Why not experiment with different ones to see which you like the best? Which of these sunflowers can you spot?

Skyscraper

15 POINTS

Teddy Bear

20 POINTS

Little Becka

20 POINTS

Strawberry Blonde

30 POINTS

Italian White

30 POINTS

Earthwalker

TOP SPOT!

40 POINTS

Create a bog garden

If an area of your garden is always damp, adapt it into a bog garden and attract just as much wildlife as a pond.

You'll need:

spade, scissors, piece of butyl liner, bog plants, gardening gloves, different-sized stones, watering can

What to do:

1 With the help of an adult, dig a hole about 30 cm deep. Make the hole the same size as your piece of butyl liner.

2 Ask an adult to cut some small holes in your liner to allow for drainage.

3 Put the piece of butyl liner in the bottom of the hole you have dug out, then put back the soil.

4 Water the area thoroughly. If possible, use rainwater to maintain the acidity of the soil.

5 Leave your bog for a few days. Then around the edges of the bog, plant bog-loving plants such as creeping jenny or marsh marigold. Lay different-sized stones in and around your bog to allow insects to safely land for a drink.

Can you i-Spy this wildlife in your bog garden?

House martin

⭐ **30** POINTS

Dragonfly larvae

⭐ **20** POINTS

Heron

⚪ **10** POINTS

Grass snake

⭐ **30** POINTS

Score 30 eco points for watering your bog garden with rainwater during the summer months and keeping it moist.

30 ECO POINTS

41

Collect rainwater

Collecting rainwater is one way to use your garden to make a positive environmental impact.

Rainwater can be used for different jobs inside and outside the home. Each litre of rainwater that you collect reduces the dependency on mains water and cuts water bills.

You'll need:

plastic bottles or buckets, scissors

What to do:

1 Look at the weather forecast and find out when it is most likely to rain in your area.

2 Choose an open patch of your garden that will have the most exposure to the rain.

3 Set up your bucket(s) or cut the top off plastic bottles and line them up so that they can collect water. You may need to place stones in the bottles to weigh them down if it is windy outside.

4 When your containers are full, store your water until it can be used in your garden or home.

How many of these jobs can you do with your collected rainwater?

Water your garden

Wash a car

Fill garden bogs, ponds and water features

Flush your toilet using filtered rainwater (ask an adult to help you find out how to filter the rainwater).

Can you think of any others?

Toilets usually use about 5-6 litres of water every time you flush. Score 30 eco points for using filtered rainwater to flush the toilet. Using rainwater instead of the mains will save lots of water and help the environment.

30 ECO POINTS

42

Create an environmentally friendly garden

Climate change is a big problem that the whole world is facing.

The UK's gardens cover a combined landmass that is bigger than the Lake District and Peak District put together – that's huge! If we all look after our gardens in a sustainable way, it really will help tackle climate change.

You'll need:

local plants, a tree, peat-free compost, paint or pens, wood to make signpost

What to do:

1. Talk to an adult about filling your garden with native plants – plants that grow naturally in the UK. Invasive species (organisms that are not native to the area) can be harmful.

2. If you have space, ask an adult if you can plant a tree. Even one tree provides huge environmental benefits for your garden and wildlife.

3. Allow a small patch of your garden to overgrow and get messy. This will give local wildlife a perfect place to be.

4. Avoid using peat. Peat is a main ingredient of compost and this has led peatlands across the UK to be damaged. Always try to use peat-free compost in your garden.

Visiting peatlands is a great way to remind yourself how important it is to conserve these areas. Peatlands form over thousands of years and are made up of dead plants that haven't quite broken down.

If you are in an area with peatlands, see if you can spot...

Bog asphodel

15 POINTS

Sphagnum moss

15 POINTS

TOP SPOT!

Golden plover

25 POINTS

Common lizard

40 POINTS

Score 25 eco points for talking with your family and friends about how peatlands are important in tackling climate change. For example, they store more carbon from the atmosphere than forests. Many plants and animals also live in peatlands; lots of them are not found in any other habitat.

25 ECO POINTS

43

Grow your own strawberries

You can either grow fruit and vegetables in a vegetable patch in your garden or in pots and containers. Strawberries are easy to grow and a perfect fruit to enjoy during summer.

You'll need:

small strawberry plants, trowel, spade, pots, compost, hay/straw, gardening gloves, watering can

What to do:

1 Fill your container or vegetable patch with compost and gently take your strawberry plants out of their pots.

2 Using the trowel, make holes that are a few centimetres deep in the compost and place your strawberry plants in them. Evenly space out your plants around the container or in the vegetable patch and water them every day. Make sure your strawberries have plenty of sunlight.

3 When the strawberries appear, you may need to cover them with a net to stop birds stealing the fruit. Lay some dry straw/hay underneath the strawberries to keep them from resting on the damp soil. The strawberries will be ripe enough to pick and eat when they are bright red.

When you are growing vegetables, remember to:
- sow your seeds in spring
- sow the seeds deep enough in the soil
- space out your seeds a good distance apart to give them space to grow
- water them regularly.

How many of these can you spot growing?

Onions

10 POINTS

Carrots

10 POINTS

Tomatoes

10 POINTS

Courgettes

10 POINTS

44

Build a home for a bat

The UK is home to 18 different species of bat. The most common is the pipistrelle bat. Sadly, many of their natural roosting sites are being disturbed or destroyed, so building your own bat house gives a safe space for a bat to sleep during the day and raise their pups.

If you aren't able to make your own bat house, you can buy a ready-made bat box from organisations like the RSPB or the Bat Conservation Trust.

You'll need:

a bat house kit, ladder, drill, stainless screws or adjustable ties

What to do:

1. With the help of an adult, look online for detailed instructions about how to make a bat house. Use untreated wood.

2. Look for a spot on a large, mature tree that is at least 3 metres from the ground. It should be exposed to the sun for a good part of the day and sheltered from strong winds.

3. Ask an adult to drill holes into the back plate of the bat house, so that you can secure it to a tree.

4 With the help of an adult, use a ladder to attach your bat house to the tree. You can use screws, or if you don't want to damage the tree, use adjustable ties.

5 Wait for bats to find their new home!

6 If you don't see bats going in and out, look on the ground for black droppings underneath the entrance to the bat house. This could indicate that bats are using it.

Bats and their homes are protected by law, so it is important when you put up your bat house that you don't disturb it and only watch from a distance.

Don't stop there! If you enjoyed this activity, why not put up more bat houses close by? Research shows that bats are more likely to roost if there are several boxes near each other.

45

Attract bats to your garden

In addition to building a bat house, there are other ways to attract bats to your garden.

What to do:

1 Plant night-scented flowers like night-flowering catchfly, sweet rocket and white jasmine. These flowers also attract night-flying insects like moths, which bats eat.

2 Keep cats indoors at night.

Keeping your cat inside at night can help protect bats. Cats often learn where bats are living and return to catch them as they leave their homes.

Once you've attracted bats to your garden, you might want to identify them. Bats are a good indicator that your outdoor space is healthy and the ecosystem is in balance.

How many of these bats can you spot?

Brown long-eared bat

25 POINTS

Common pipistrelle bat

25 POINTS

Soprano pipistrelle bat

35 POINTS

Daubenton's bat

TOP SPOT!

40 POINTS

Score 30 eco points for recording bat sightings to the Bat Conservation Trust, an organisation that keeps track of UK bat populations.

30 ECO POINTS

Make a moth trap

There are many more species of moth than butterfly in the UK: many of them are nocturnal (active at night). Setting up a moth trap at night is your best chance to spot them. Don't worry, the moths are not harmed in the trap.

You'll need:

an old white bedsheet, pegs, torch, notebook and pen

What to do:

1 With the help of an adult, just before nightfall peg an old white bedsheet outside, over a washing line, tree branch or between garden chairs.

2 Set up a torch nearby so the light shines directly onto the hanging sheet.

3 Watch as different species of moth are attracted to the torch light and land on the bedsheet. Be patient as it may take some time to see moths.

4 Try to identify the moths that are caught in your trap – describe them or draw them in a notebook. How many species can you spot in a single night?

Moths are extremely important insects in the environment. They are pollinators and prey to other insects, amphibians and mammals.

Which of these species can you spot in your moth trap?

Scarlet tiger
30 POINTS

Green carpet
20 POINTS

Large emerald
25 POINTS

Angle shades
20 POINTS

Magpie
35 POINTS

Hummingbird hawk
40 POINTS

TOP SPOT!

Listen to wildlife noises at night

Many animals are active at night. Although they might be harder to spot than wildlife during the day, you may be able to hear them in their search for food or a mate.

You'll need:

blanket, recorder, notepad and pen, torch

What to do:

1 Ask permission from an adult to stay up a little later than normal and make yourself comfortable beside a window or in your back garden. Remember to wrap up warm if it is cold outside.

2 Stay quiet and listen carefully for any noises.

3 Record any noises you hear or write a detailed description of what time you heard the noise and what animal you think it may be.

Have you ever heard a high-pitched scream in the night during winter? It could be a fox trying to attract a mate. It sounds like a baby screeching.

Did you know that the 'too-wit too-woo' noise of an owl is actually two tawny owls? The female owl makes the 'too-wit' noise and the male answers with the 'too-woo'.

If you hear loud grunting and snuffling, it could mean that a hedgehog is close by, sniffing out tasty earthworms and slugs.

Frogs croak loudly at night – to attract a mate during the breeding season or to defend their territory. Listen out for a noise that sounds like a rumbling growl.

Nightjars migrate from Africa and arrive in the UK between late April to mid-May. They spend the summer in the UK before flying back to Africa in September. These nocturnal birds are known for a loud 'coo-ick' call that you are likely to hear most around dusk.

Watch the wildlife in your garden

To watch wildlife at night in your garden, you need to set up a camera. You don't need to have a big, expensive camera to capture footage – you can use a phone or webcam.

You'll need:

wildlife camera/webcam/mobile phone

What to do:

1 Before you put a camera or phone outside, you need to do a few checks with an adult. If you are using a wildlife camera, make sure an adult knows how to set it up correctly. If you are using a phone, make sure it is in a protective case and the video is recording in night mode.

2 Make sure your equipment is fully charged and has enough memory to store footage until morning.

3 Ask an adult to securely attach the camera about waist height to a tree or fence post. Then test it is recording.

4 To get great close-up footage, try placing some food or water near to your camera.

A wildlife hide lets you watch the natural behaviour of animals that visit your garden without them knowing you are there. You can make a wildlife hide by draping a bedsheet over poles/branches.

See if you can spot these creatures from your wildlife hide.

Fox
20 POINTS

Chiffchaff
30 POINTS

Woodmouse
25 POINTS

Badger
30 POINTS

Score 30 eco points for finding out about camera traps. They offer a new way to see and learn about wildlife and help us appreciate the natural world.

30 ECO POINTS

Clean your gardening tools

When all the winter jobs are finished in your garden, give your gardening tools a good clean and store them away until spring. Keeping your tools clean and in good condition helps prevent disease in your garden.

You'll need:

bucket, soapy water, cloth or sponge, towel, lubricant/rust-proof spray

What to do:

1 With the help of an adult, fill a bucket with warm, soapy water.

2 Give the gardening tools a good wash with a cloth or sponge. Remember, tools can be sharp, so make sure an adult is with you when you wash them. Always clean one tool at a time.

3 Lay your washed tools on an old towel and thoroughly dry them.

3 When your tools are completely dry, ask an adult to help you spray them with a rust-proof spray or lubricant (something like WD-40). This will stop your tools becoming rusty or sticky when you use them again.

Make your own bubbles

Create your own soapy mixture and blow bubbles into the breeze! Ask an adult to help you with this activity.

You'll need:

cup, bowl, spoon, warm water, liquid soap, scissors, a straw/ recycled plastic bottle

What to do:

1 Into a bowl pour five cups of warm water and one cup of liquid soap. Slowly stir until the liquid soap has dissolved.

2 Use a straw as your bubble wand. Or ask an adult to help you recycle a plastic bottle by carefully cutting it in two with scissors. Save the top half.

3 Carry your bowl to an outside space and put it on a flat surface.

4 Dip the bottom of your straw or halved bottle into the soapy mixture and slowly swirl it around.

5 Pull it out of the bowl. Then blow on the straw or bottleneck to produce bubbles!

Index

Take on the other i-SPY challenges!

Discover more fun and fascinating i-SPY books at collins.co.uk/i-SPY